the mosaic
of my
becoming

by

justine capuson

Copyright © 2020 by Justine Capuson

For permission requests, contact the publisher at:
www.Holon.co

ISBN#: 978-0-9966685-2-1

Published by:

Holon Publishing & Collective Press
A Storytelling Company
www.Holon.co

Visit the author's website for future publications, updates, and more:

www.justinecapuson.com

the mosaic
of my
becoming

by
justine capuson

the euphoria

you are made of the earth
and i am made of fire

i simply could not breathe
without you

　　　　- compatibility

how does she do it?
that moon

standing alone, so confident
so strong

amid a sea of absence
of darkness

when i cannot
go one night
without being held

by you

-insomnia

our hands intertwined
as you gently placed the syringe
inside of me

and with each pump
of its nectar
the wilting subsided

until my breath escaped me
and i finally bloomed

-on the first night of love

how ironic it is
that your spontaneity

is the binding
that holds me together

-muse

i long
for the scent of your skin

because it reminds me
of being home

-redolence

it was our first real argument

the flowers wilted as they looked on
anxiously
awaiting the final blow

when suddenly
your cold demeanor subsided

as you took my defeated face
cheeks flushed with the hours of tears
anger
exhaustion

and softly whispered

enough, my love
put that suitcase back in the closet
where it belongs

and come here

-i crave our lows, too

i could have sworn
that pink tulip
over there

just told the sun
she envied me

-so i tightened my grip on your hand

how strange it is
that you are able to expose me

without placing those hands
anywhere near my body

-the unravelling

justine capuson

tell me
why i crave you even more

at your worst

-vice

when the magnets in our souls collided
my heart untethered and thrusted towards you
as if it were returning to its rightful home

at a loss, i ran after it
trying to protect its innocent eyes
from witnessing

the electric, dangerous beauty
of your aura

until finally my lungs failed me
and i surrendered my self
to the divinity of your existence

-infatuation

your eyes reveal a subtle pain
as if
they're tethered to the pillars
of your scars

but in the most divine
way possible

-*fixer upper*

you are the vein
that pumps meaning

into my existence

   -salvation

the books
i once treasured
now collect dust

for my mind
has no time

it is simply too occupied
with the stunning visions

of us

-lost

on the third ring
i motioned towards it

as you looked at me
irritated by the interruption
partially confused

and as i withdrew my reach
it dawned on me

that you were right

i did not need anybody
besides you

-draw the blinds

my mother once told me

there are three signs
that indicate a good heart

> 1. he loves his mother
> 2. he loves animals
> 3. he has passion

you check off all three

-honey hues

i love
how you stay awake

to blow out the candle

after
i've fallen asleep

- lavender

i take solace
in your vulnerability

-3:30 am

my eyes filled with humiliation
the first time
your fingertips traced the scars
on my winding hips

these scars, a sign of growth, of strength
are a part of your femininity
you should never feel ashamed

you whispered

as you ever so gently
laid me down in the silk sheets

-the falling

please tell me the name
of the star

who sculpted your soul
from the sun

-so i can send her a thank you card

how on earth
did i survive two decades

without the sound of your voice

-pillow talk

i trust you

i do

but tell me
why each fluttering stride
of her ornate, jasmine wings
sends my heart into a panic

aching with envy
betrayal

at the sheer thought
that something so irresistible
so beautiful

could be on its way
to you

-paranoia

i beg the universe
each night

to never take you
away from me

-bedtime ritual

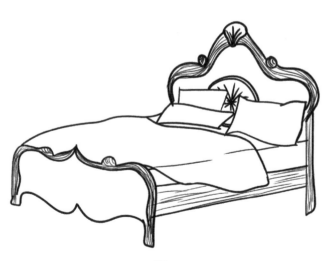

there is nothing
more breathtaking

than your tears

-vulnerability

you held the book in one hand
and graced my palm with the other

so i sat quietly

mesmerized by the intricate pattern
of the winding ridges
branded
on the surface of your thumb

-how can such perfect dna exist

i drew the curtains of my eyes
to greet the morning sun

when i felt the tips of my eye lashes
sweep away
the scars on your heart

-to wake up with my head on your chest

my god, how i love to watch
your morning routine

so meticulous
yet never mundane

-to love a virgo

you surrendered to the moon
just moments before me

your eyelids peacefully drawn
but your subconscious slowly awakening

and my heart quietly wept
because *yes* you were mine

but i'd never fully know you
unless i could somehow gain access

to those dreams

  - the gate keeper

i exhausted the clocks
envisioning the day
the universe would take me
to my soulmate

but no amount
of manifestation
could have prepared me
for you

- *diary entry no.18*

i caught a glimpse of the morning sun
having the audacity
to take her lips
and trace the outline of your face

so i quickly shut the blinds
before you could witness her beauty

and pulled your body
tightly
into mine

> *- you always told me you loved my*
> *possessiveness*

the erosion

i promise, my love
i won't make a fuss

if you'd just tell me
i'm not wrong

that in order to be with you
i must tether my voice
to the weight of cement

and suffocate it
in the depths of the sea

-drowning

on the second night
i drained the vase
cleansed its crystal body

and watched in awe
as the lilies, too

could no longer breathe
without you

-broken

for every red flag ignored
take the sharp, silver blade

and flush one teaspoon of crimson water
from beneath your flesh
down the drain

    -the masochist

the flowers that once envied me

now bow their heads
in shame

-discarded

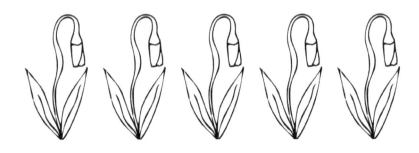

it started out with denial

awakening to your gentle touch
only to discover
that the gold beads draped over your nightstand
boasted shiny initials that were not my own

he's lying to you
my gut warned
as you pulled me close to your chest
reassuring me i was the only one

until one day, the pain buried deep in my gut
surfaced
into black and blue marble
splattered across the canvas of my arms, my wrists, my ribs

how can a man who loves you cause you so much pain?
my gut wept
as you took my tired face
into the bittersweet palms of your hands
and whispered

i love you; i'll never hurt you again

   -addiction

if my spirit was sculpted
from fire

why do i feel
like i am drowning

-aries

i fasted
for seven days

and gained pleasure
as my stomach wept

this is your punishment
i told her

because it is your fault he left

-this mirror no longer has any use

for so long

i confused listening
with submission

-abuse is not always black and blue

please
just guide my hand
to the same switch you used

to turn off your feelings
for me

-teach me how to detach

on the second ring, her heart breaks in two
as if it were her, twenty-five years ago
navigating the uncertainty of self-worth all over again

you feel shame as you quietly mutter the words
but he promised it would be different this time…

momentarily you seek solace in the warmth of her silence
awaiting the validation
the reassurance
the encouragement

until the strength in her voice echoes
the resounding truth
you've neglected to acknowledge all along

there are no victims here…
only volunteers

-a mother's wisdom

you took my trembling hand as you awaited my response
but the crippling dominance in your stare
imprisoned the words

that almost choked me
trying to get out

    -i have forgotten the sound of this voice

falling in love with you
meant falling out of love

with myself

-your favorite kind of monogamy

starvation feels no different
than the agony

of one-sided love

-hunger pains

each night i pray
that if i lose the weight
grow these locks beneath my breast

you'll one day catch a glimpse, on a crowded street

and filled with regret
come back to me

   -just tell me what i need to change

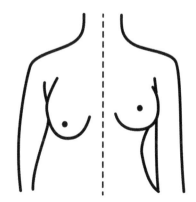

i can survive losing you
but not to somebody else

-possession

i'm not sure
which one causes more damage
to the human heart

the leaving
or the coming back

    -your favorite game

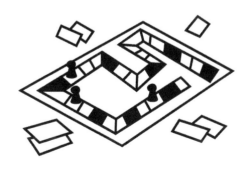

he touches me
and i pretend it is you

-the imitation

the longer i silenced
each inkling

the deeper i carved the blade
into these wounds

-denial

your footsteps grew fainter
as my heart gasped for air

slowly drowning
in the flood of each memory

-abandonment

when the heart begs you to stay
but the head begs to flee

the spirit suffers
a slow and painful
erosion

    -incongruity

the silhouette of empty promises
sculpt the scars
on your captivating, amaranth lips

each breathtaking word
injecting poison inside of me
to mask the crushing realization

that you never had any
intention to stay

-manipulation

justine capuson

how cruel it is
that we are both
the source and the threat

to our happiness

-september 28th

i heard a stranger in passing
utter the word
no
and for a brief moment
it sounded foreign to me

> *-perhaps because it's been so long
> since i've used it*

what a shame it is
that we are so quick to confuse peace
with boredom

-self-sabotage

my heart
can no longer tell

if it misses you
or me

-so it begs my head for the answers

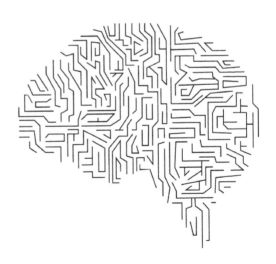

how can i move forward
if i never want to let go

of the past

-attachment

you loosened your grip
around my waist
as you looked me in the eyes

why do you want to be with someone so broken?

i felt my heart shatter
as my gut wept in shame

because for a brief moment
as i stared back into your hopeless eyes

i thought i had already fixed you

-defeat

they make it look so easy
the sun and the moon

for their existence is intertwined
but they can still stand
alone

   -co-dependency

my heart collapsed on the floor
blood-stained glass scattered across the hardwood
as i watched your lips unleash the unthinkable

the words became mute as they dripped from your tongue
but instead of begging you to stay
i slowly reached for the broom

to sweep the sharp fragments
that now cut deep
into my lungs

       -there is no such thing as closure

the morning
after you left

i replaced your touch
with the water's

and when the steam subsided
i stood, weak
frail
expired

as i stared back into the hollow reflection
of a complete
and utter stranger

-alienated

how cruel it is
that i am stuck with you

when all i want
is him

-*what i'd give to escape this flesh*

does it ever really matter
what occupies an illusion

if its true inhabitant
does not wish to be discovered

-the narcissist

he compliments me
and i crave your abuse

-stockholm syndrome

justine capuson

there is nothing more devastating
to the human heart

than the realization

you're holding on to something
that simply
no longer exists

      -unrequited

you beg me to come back
only so i can watch

you leave

-the cycle

tell me
what does she smell like?

i'm in need
of a new perfume

    -masquerade

i never thought
i'd seek comfort

in the universe's tears

-the void

there is an art
to mastering the breakup

you see
when your heart is betrayed
it shatters

and you are suddenly left with the task
of picking up a million pieces

so you can either
choose to sweep the fragments
under the rug
where their sharp edges will linger
or
you can study, mend each piece
take the glue stick
and strategically intertwine it
with the others

to create a more beautiful, ornate, vibrant
version of what the heart was
before it broke
in the first place

-*the mosaic*

the petal softly wept
as she released her tight grip

and surrendered
to the wind

-the letting go

the epiphany

on the night you left

the universe baptized my spirit

    -re-birth

the beautiful discrepancy
between incompatibility and death

is that one solidifies a permanent end to our purpose
while the other propels us toward it

   - breakups do not have to break us

loneliness can be misleading
because it challenges
its implication

you see

you can sleep
next to the man you call home
and shiver in the bitterness of abandonment
or
you can awake
in the middle of the bed
and blossom in the warmth of the sun

-appearance vs. reality

the beautiful thing about pain
that we often overlook

is the unparalleled ability
for its temporary discomfort
to cause permanent growth

-triumph

if letting go were an art
there would be more than one way
but what they don't tell you about goodbyes
is the singularity of closure

it was never about them
and always about you

accepting that sometimes
people are simply not always meant
to take permanent shelter

in the home
that is your heart

-eviction

you should never feel
that your lack of control

over the heart of someone else
is a threat to your happiness

- *disarming anxiety*

show me the meaning of love
she begged the universe
as she surrendered her soul to the stars

only to awake with the sun
illuminating the white silk sheets
that softly bandaged the scars on her winding curves

wrapped in the familiar touch
of the bed's only occupant

-april 1st

the only way to move forward
is to confront our brokenness

and conquer what pulled us backward

-accountability

why is it
that we search for answers
everywhere

but within ourselves

-introspection

you speak to the universe
using perfectly sculpted, censored words
out of fear of karma's retaliation

when in reality
you lie awake at night
silently intertwining your peace
with the small thread of hope

that he is unhappy
that he is lost without you
that he searches for your face in the crowds on the streets
…that he will come back to you

but what you must learn
is that your happiness depends
solely on your ability
to love nothing

as if it were yours
to keep

-vanity

emotions are temporary
emotions are temporary
emotions are temporary

-left hemisphere

how ironic it is
that the present

could not exist
without the past

-trust the process

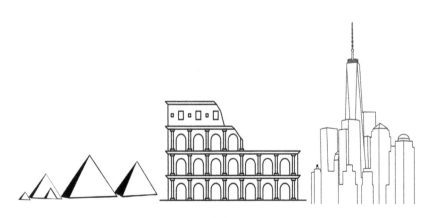

justine capuson

a life without boundaries
is no life at all

-temple

you will know
when you have found
the right love

because the simplicity
of it all
will vanish any doubts
about your worthiness

you will know
when you have found
the right love

because the endless laughter
the routine morning coffee runs
the mindless moments of intimacy
will shed weight from the heaviness
of your tainted heart

you will know
when you have found
the right love

when you can confidently say
you whole heartedly admire
the person you are becoming
because of it

-home

there is nothing more beautiful
than remaining vulnerable

in a world of insensitivity

   -empathy

and in a world of 8 billion
we beg the universe to unveil 1 soul mate

eyes desperately studying each unfamiliar face
in a roaring crowd

longing for the connection
searching for the spark

when all along
the only soul that ever needed discovery
was our own

-self-discovery

we could all be writers
if we just took the time

to embrace the vulnerability
of studying our scars

-we all have a story to tell

justine capuson

for those of you doubting
your ability to practice self-love

ask yourself
if you are capable

of saying
no

-two letter empowerment

it took

the aroma of warm vanilla
emanating from pastry shops
in venice, florence, and rome

countless walks along the graffitied canals
of the roaring london fish market

the fascination of each local
pensively surveying art
in the ornate parisian cafes

the sweet scent of morning dew
as i watched the sun
greet the sleepy streets of edinburgh

all the way to the vibrant
infinite mediterranean shores
of barcelona and the costa rican lush

to truly see, for the first time
that my purpose in this world
was so much greater
than simply settling
for you

-buy the plane ticket

we search so desperately for romantic partners
that we overlook the unparalleled beauty

of our friends

-L.K

you will know
if he loves you back

you will know

**-that's the beautiful thing about
reciprocity**

the stars were intentional
when they graced you
with the ability to feel deeply

never feel ashamed
of the gift
that is your sensitivity

-the well

we underestimate the strength
of the human heart

the inherent part of us
that will never survive this world
unscathed

for it will wither and tear
shatter and burst

but it will never
surrender

it will instead silently grow
into its new form

and you will know when it mends
because your soul, too

will heal with it

-the healing

you cannot love somebody
you do not trust

you cannot love somebody
you do not trust

you cannot love somebody
you do not trust

you cannot love somebody
you do not trust

-lessons from jean

we must prove
that we can conquer the dark

in order to receive the light

- *the sun and the moon*

when a vulnerable heart is shattered
the mind injects poison
to numb us from the pain of the unfathomable

he left you because you were too needy
he cheated on you because you were not enough
he hit you because you were in the wrong

when in reality
the universe bows its head
takes our trembling hand and whispers

his actions are a reflection of him
and say absolutely nothing
about you

> *- **actions are mirrors, too***

it was our tenth session

what is it that you miss, exactly?
is it the lying?
the cheating?
the bruises that covered your arms?

my words failed me
as i tightened the grip
between the chair and my two sweaty palms

what you fear
is being alone

trust me
you do not miss that man
at all

-book the therapy appointment

timelines are not meant
to be uniform

-the odyssey

instead of resenting abandonment
for ordering the massacre on your heart

you must understand
that the aches, the tears, the wales

are merely the universe's way of whispering

ah, but what you cannot see yet
is that your life has only
just begun

> ***-everything happens for a reason***

i stared in awe
at the vibrant explosion
of each unfolding petal
bursting in amaranth and tangerine

but what i could not grasp
as i stood blinded by its immaculate beauty
were how its roots
such an inherent part of its existence
stretched deep beneath the surface

permanently embedded
in the darkest
muddiest waters of the pond

-nymphaea nelumbo (indian lotus)

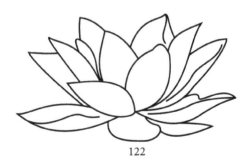

and suddenly it dawned on me
that it was never about what i did or did not do

because he'd never be happy
with *anyone*
until he was truly happy

with himself

    -3:24 am

if only we trusted with conviction
that the universe
deliberately gives and takes

we would save ourselves
the agony
the heartbreak
the anxiety

of searching

for something
for someone

a search that was never
ours to control
in the first place

-intentional impermanence

i began to feel sorry for him

because the saddest thing about a liar
is the false reality in which they live

-i hope one day you heal, too

you must always remember
that there is no greater salvation
than envisioning the day

you cross paths with the person
who was carved out of this earth's flesh

to whole heartedly love you
exactly
as you are

-manifestation

the extraordinary thing about the wrong kind of love
is its ability to guide us

one step closer
to the right one

-february 15th

before you question the universe's intentions
for continuing to place toxic people on your path

you must write a list of all the boundaries
you've firmly set, and kept, in place

and if your pen does not move
you already have your answer

>   *-you must fix yourself, first, and the
>   rest will follow suit*

your first great love
may not manifest
in affection towards another human being

you see
when you have discovered your purpose
it will infiltrate your dreams

instilling restlessness at night
you will eagerly await the sun

to mark one more day
that you are able to unwrap
the gift

that sits patiently
at your fingertips

   -passion

the only way
to truly heal
is to delve head-first into the heartbreak
and study each scar

for they will tell you
with conviction

what you will *never*
tolerate again

-the rebuilding

justine capuson

you are worthy
and deserving
of a love that does *not* complete you

but instead
gives you the space
the courage
the motivation
the support

to become
your own
home

-balance

you must trust that you are not alone
as you feel gutted, isolated, exhausted
on the verge of surrendering to the pain
of yet another loss

you see, the extraordinary people like you
who have the most love to give
are the ones who suffer the deepest wounds

you must trust that you are rare
that the people in this world who need your love the most
the ones your magnetic soul attracts
are the people who were never capable of reciprocating
the warmth in your touch
the tenderness in your heart
the calming nature of your very existence
in the first place

you must trust that this pain
is not a defining feature of who you are

but instead is a sign
that the universe is pulling you away from the people
who intended to weaken the strength in your vibration
the strength this world so desperately needs

you must trust that this loss
is bringing you one step closer
to the greatest love you've ever known

and in an infinite universe
it is a gift
it is a miracle
that i am able
to exist at the same time as you

this world needs your heart
this world needs your vulnerability
this world needs your love

-an ode to the empath

it gives me satisfaction
to know

that when you've outgrown her
you will regret losing me

-to the boy from the bay area

justine capuson

take a deep breath
and truly ask yourself

will this matter in two hours? three weeks?
four months? five years?

-the golden rule

my favorite mornings
are the rainy ones

when the universe
sheds its tears
to soothe its wounds, its scars
with the nectar
of new life

it's on these mornings
that i take one scoop of cocoa butter
and gently feed my own scars
the ones that outline my hips, my waist, my thighs

for these scars are the living proof
of how much change, how much pain, how much growth
the female body can endure

without breaking

> **-morning ritual**

healing is not the sudden realization
that awakens your soul
as you desperately search for answers
in a guide to self-love

healing does not manifest
within retreating to the comfort of your past
because the questions that haunt you at night
instill fear in your dreams about the future

healing is not the final destination
in the journey to self-discovery
the destination you long for
as you envy the sun for kissing his skin

don't you see?

healing is the culmination of every mindless moment
that is the act of living
the very confrontation of being alone

healing is the silhouette of you dancing
in the kitchen of your tiny apartment
unable to identify the catalyst
of the warmth that suddenly ignites your bones

healing is knowing, with conviction, when it is time to let go
time to reach deep into your past
not to retreat to the person who once felt like home
but to gather and plant the seeds
of every lesson you learned along the way

healing is forgiving
forgiving yourself for pouring every ounce of your love
into the heart of someone who was never capable
of feeding yours in return

healing is recognizing your worth
the understanding that it was never about
what you could or could not give to them
what you did or did not do for them

healing is the ability to trust
that the heart break
the betrayal
the loss
the weight of the crushing realizations
led you to this exact moment

because your purpose has always been
to *become*
and not
to *be*

-what they don't tell you about healing

justine capuson

these vulnerable pages
hold each delicate fragment
of the mosaic
that is my identity

the twenty-four years
of euphoria
erosion

and the epiphanies
that slowly healed
my heart

-the becoming

you always promised me
this day would come

    -to my incredible mother, the very
    essence of female strength

about the author

justine capuson, author of *the mosaic of my becoming*, views herself and her life as a reflection of the vibrant, complex, rough-edged fragments of survival- the fleeting moments of loving, breaking, and becoming- the breathtaking spaces in between.

justine's 2020 debut book, a three-part poetry collection, showcases her unique ability to capture the depth of human emotion through simplistic poetic structure, illustrations, and words. the collection, inspired by her own self-discovery journey, explores a variety of themes ranging from love, abandonment, loss, femininity, healing, and becoming.

soon after completing her degree in english studies, justine began teaching creative writing and world literature. the author's poetry, rooted in her lifelong fascination with storytelling, is intended to inspire those who find themselves in the thick of life's uncertainty, slowly piecing together the ornate fragments of their own mosaic identity.